Baby Names

A Simple Guide to Picking the Perfect Name Including Thousands of Names with Meaning and Origin

Contents

PART 1: A Guide to Choosing Baby Names: Everything You Need to Know

Introduction

Congratulations on this new chapter in your life! Before you officially enter into this crazy journey known as parenthood, prior to the arrival of endless crying and dirty diapers, you have a very important task to accomplish: choosing a name for your baby.

Deciding what to name your child is one of the most difficult and most important decisions you may ever make. After all, it sets the tone for his or her life! You don't want to give your child a name that is embarrassing or overly difficult to pronounce, and you certainly don't want them to have a name with a double meaning or mortifying translation. This guide will take you step by step through the process of choosing a baby name, from what to avoid to what's trending.

Choosing the Perfect Name

Unfortunately, there's no one-size-fits-all formula for choosing the perfect baby name. A lot of the process depends on your preferences, traditions, and expectations. If you go into the baby naming process knowing you want a two-syllable girl's name that starts with an "S", this process will likely go a lot faster than if you were waiting to be surprised with the gender and are going into the process with no parameters.

Lucky for you, regardless of where you're at in the process, we've got you covered. Even if you think you already know what you want to name your son or daughter, there's no harm in making sure you don't make a mistake you might not even realize is a mistake. If you're certain about a name, make sure it follows all the things you should keep in mind, avoids any pitfalls, and falls in line with the final checklist. This guide is here to help you narrow your focus and avoid making a name mistake that will stay with your child for the rest of his or her life. We're here to make sure you choose the perfect name!

What to Keep in Mind When Choosing Your Baby's Name

The Popularity Factor

It happens... we hear a name we like on a TV show, or at the playground, or in a restaurant. It's easy to get stuck on a name and decide that that's the name your child is going to have, but do your research first. If you heard the name, that means at least one other person in your area has the name. There's a chance it could be a unique name you just happened to overhear, or it could be one of the most popular baby names this year.

Names like Ava and Emma are adorable, but your daughter is bound to have two neighbors named Ava and four friends at her daycare named Emma, so you might want to think twice before giving your child a popular name. Noah has topped the list of popular boys' names for the past four years. Unless you want your son to share his name with thousands of others his age, opt against Noah until the popularity fades a bit.

Studies have even been done that found that nearly half of the parents who regret the name they gave their child feel that way because the name got way too popular. Do some research and ask a few close friends—especially those with young kids in daycare and school— their thoughts. If this is your first child, or you haven't had children in the past three or five years, you might be out of touch with the current trends. Names that were popular when you were a kid are likely old news now, and names that you might think are unique could be topping all the baby name lists.

How Has It Been Used?

While naming after pop culture characters and celebrities is very on-trend right now (more about that later), consider how ordinary names are used in pop culture before deciding on those names for your child. For example, you may love the name Miley for a girl, but know that she will undoubtedly be asked at least once a week for the rest of her life if she's named after Miley Cyrus. If you're crazy about the name Stephanie but are looking for a unique spelling and opt for Stefani, you will constantly be asked if you're a big Gwen Stefani fan.

Along the same lines, you certainly don't want to choose a name that is associated with negativity. Obvious examples include Adolf, Osama, Ted, or any "O" name with a middle name or prefix that would result in them being called "OJ". You might want to go so far as to not naming after any fictional villains, like Lord Voldemort from the *Harry Potter* series or Cruella deVil from *101 Dalmatians*.

Potential Nicknames

You certainly don't want to choose a name that just has a bunch of awful puns or rhymes waiting around the corner. We've all been through middle school and high school and know how cruel kids can be.   Consider any possible nicknames or rhymes that can develop from the name you like to ensure that other children don't have a nice laugh at the expense of your child's name.

For example, the name Chuck rhymes with some words that aren't so nice and you probably wouldn't want other kids using in reference to your child. There's also Fatty

Patty, Harry who's Hairy, Icky Vicky, Smelleanor, Smelliott... the list goes on! Go through the alphabet and make sure the name(s) you like don't have any unfortunate rhymes, and take to the internet to do a quick search on whether or not there are any not-so-great nicknames for your chosen name(s).

Pronunciation is Key

Let's not beat around the bush. To go along with refraining from giving your child a name that is completely unheard of or ridiculous, don't give your child a name that is difficult to pronounce. Sure, there are people everywhere that can mispronounce names as simple as Michael or Kristin, but don't make it any harder on your child than it has to be. If their name is pronounced as Kylie, there is no need to spell it Khileighe. If you want a unique spelling, maybe go for something that is different from the normal Kylie but still can be read without missing a beat, like Kiley or Kyleigh.

This is something that can impact your child from the time they're born until they're in their sixties and beyond. It's simple: have some people read the name as you want to spell it, and make sure that at least 90% of them read it correctly at first glance. If you're set on giving your child a unique name that no one else has, by no means, go for it! Please just make sure it's easily pronounceable.

We don't mean to scare you if the name you love is just a bit different, because what we're talking about is simply absurd spelling and made up names. Let's take a look at some of the names we're talking about:

- Maaike
- Kuyler
- Saoirse
- Chiwetel
- Ioan
- Anais
- Merewen
- Kaia

If you're set on a name like Siobhan, Schuyler, or Isla, you'll also have to accept the fact that you and your child will be subject to answering pronunciation questions at least once a day for the rest of your/their lives.

Remember That They Grow Up

This is a big one that not a lot of parents think about. Sure, a six-month-old girl named Charlie or Lily is cute, but what about a 40-year-old with the same name? When naming a child, most people don't think about how the name will impact them for years to come, but it's a name they're stuck with forever. Picture them in high school, college, and beyond. If you would be embarrassed to have a name at any of those ages, you probably shouldn't make your child endure it.

Nicknames are the best solution to this problem. Instead of naming your son Johnny, name him Jonathan and simply call him Johnny when he's young. As he gets older, he can decide what he wants to be called. You can always use nicknames that change with age, so consider going with Charlotte and calling her Charlie when she's young, then switching to Charlotte as she gets older. If you give your child a name like Ellie, Davey, or Izzy, they're stuck with the name as they get older, so consider that before opting for a name because it's "cute"!

The Big Picture

How does the first name you chose sound with your last name? This isn't necessarily a deal breaker, but remember that, in school, it's not uncommon for students to be called by their first and last name. Don't make your child be the one who always has to answer to "John Johnson". In addition to making sure it doesn't sound ridiculous, make sure that the combination doesn't result in anything inappropriate. Someone with the last name Shaw probably wouldn't be well off naming their child Richard, as it is often shortened to "Rick" and he would be Rick Shaw (rickshaw). Now this might not bother you, but it's definitely something to keep in mind when deciding on a name.

Along the same lines are initials. This is a big mistake some people don't realize until it's too late to fix. Before finalizing your decision, look at your child's first, middle, and last initials put together. Does it spell something embarrassing? Is it a curse word? You definitely don't want your child's initials spelling "ASS" or "MAD" or "STD".

Traditions

As we'll go into further detail on in a few chapters, there are important traditions you might want to consider when naming your child, from religious traditions to familial traditions. These can include giving your child a certain name, using a particular first letter to fit in with the family or name after the dead, and/or naming your child within the guidelines of your religious beliefs. Speak to family members about any customs in your family or religion before you fall in love with a name that doesn't quite fit!

Compatibility

This is it… your baby boy, Asher James, is about to be born. You've had his name picked out for months. Here he is…but wait! He doesn't *look* like an Asher! It happens. People realize the name they've chosen doesn't suit their newborn child. This is something that not everyone cares about, so it's up to you to decide if you want to have a list of alternative names, or even not decide on the name until you see the baby. Otherwise, you can just stick with Asher and hope he grows into it! If there's any one point on this list for you to not worry about, this is the one. Compatibility of a name is important, but it's also a matter of opinion.

Pitfalls to Avoid

Popularity vs. Uniqueness

So, we said that you shouldn't pick a name that's overly popular. But what about a name that's too unique? Believe it or not, there is such a thing. Growing up with a name like Jessica or Michael in the 1990s or Isabella or Aiden in the current decade isn't easy. However, growing up with a name that no one has ever heard before can be equally as difficult. Have you ever met a kid named Igor, Pinky, Verity, or Lysander? Probably not, and there's a reason for it. Spare your child the trouble of having to repeat their name five times and explain the meaning anytime someone asks their name.

This goes hand in hand with the pronunciation issue, as you don't want your child to have to explain the pronunciation or explain the name itself. If you have to ask yourself if the name is "too unique", chances are that it is. It differs in that there could be a name that everyone can pronounce, like Uranus or Brassiere, that falls into the category of being too odd to work as a baby name. This leads us to our next point...

Naming After Inanimate Objects

As tempting as it may be to look around the room and pick an object to name over, please do not do it! This is a trend that is popular amongst celebrities. Gwyneth Paltrow has a daughter named Apple, while Ashley Parker Angel named his child Lyric. Kelly Clarkson and Jamie Oliver both have daughters named River. Oliver's daughter's middle name is even Rocket. It may seem cute now, but imagine meeting a 30-year-old woman named Apple. Undoubtedly, the first thought that would pop into your mind would be, "What were her parents thinking?".

In addition to celebrities, average folks have been giving their children names like Mars, Lion, Strawberry, Moon, and Valentine. No child wants to go through life wondering why their parents decided to name them after a fruit or planet. If an object's name hasn't been used as a name for a child before, there's probably a good reason, so it's best to skip it altogether.

Switching and Adding Letters

There can only be so many names in the world, so it's sort of expected that variations of different names become their own names as time goes on. Instead of just Hayden or Aiden, there's also Brayden, Kayden, and Jaden, all of which have become popular boys' names in recent years.

The same goes with girls' names like Allison evolving into Addison and Adeline, and Emily evolving into Emma and Emmaline. These are all gorgeous names that are a spin on a typical name but easy to pronounce. If you're looking for uniqueness, consider variations of a common name that still result in another understandable, pronounceable name.

With that being said, there is a line that shouldn't be crossed. Don't give your child an absurd name just because the name you like is too common. If you like Riley but think it's too popular of a name, don't just switch and make it Raley or Siley. This will just confuse everyone. Check out this list below of name variations that didn't end up so great for the child:

- Miracle → Dmiracle
- Dalton → Dolton
- Maximus → Maximum
- Sydney → Cydnee
- Alan → Jallen
- Jason → Kayson
- Adrian → Da'Dreian

Yes, believe it or not, these are all names that have actually been given to children. Stay away from inventing names just for the sake of trying to be different.

Poor Name Meaning

Name meanings can both positively and negatively impact your decision on what to name your child. This is definitely a matter of personal preference, but it's something to keep in the back of your mind. If you have a name, or several names, that you love, it's up to you to decide if the meaning of the name will affect whether or not you choose the name for your child.

Let's go through a list of some of the seemingly most adorable names and their not-so-great meanings:

- Cecelia- Blind, dim-witted
- Claudia- Lame
- Lilith- Night monster
- Molly- Bitter
- Calvin- Bald
- Brennan- Sorrow
- Cameron- Crooked nose
- Campbell- Crooked mouth
- Mallory- Unfortunate
- Gideon- Stump for a hand
- Portia- Pig
- Kennedy- Deformed head
- Olivia- Elf army

On the other hand, there are names you might be considering whose meanings might seal the deal. Check out these gorgeous names with just as equally gorgeous meanings:

- Sophia- Wise
- Caroline- Song of happiness
- Victoria- Triumphant
- Jolie- Cheerful
- Ellie- Shining light
- Ethan - Strong
- Alexander- Defender
- Aaron- Enlightened, mountain of strength
- Noah- Comfort
- Ace- Number one

Real talk: A name meaning, for the most part, isn't make-it-or-break-it when it comes to deciding on a name for your child. The reality is, most people don't even know what their own name means. However, it definitely *is* something to consider, as it could upset your child down the line. If you've narrowed down the two possible choices for your son to Calvin and Aaron, and Calvin means "bald" while Aaron means "enlightened", it may shift your decision toward Aaron.

What it comes down to for all of these things to remember and pitfalls to avoid is **common sense**. If you tell people your potential name and they laugh or cringe, it probably isn't a good choice. If you text message a bunch of friends the name you've chosen and they have to call to have you pronounce it for them, you should probably choose a different spelling or move onto the next name. Your child's name is the first thing that defines them when they're born, so make sure you pick a name not because it's unheard of or catchy, but because it is a good choice for them.

Different Baby Naming Traditions

Many people have different traditions or customs they follow when deciding what to name their child, so this is definitely something to keep in mind. Some of these customs are religious, others are generational, and there are those that are simply a new tradition being started. These are some examples of traditions you might want to consider, and, remember, it's never too late to start your own tradition!

Naming After the Dead

Let's start with the most common tradition, naming after a loved one who has passed away. Many people find that this is a great way to honor someone's memory. In some religions, such as Judaism, this is customary. For example, if your grandfather named Samuel passed away when you were young, you might name your daughter Samantha. This tradition can be factored into your decision by making a list of loved ones you would consider naming your child after and going from there. Some people choose to use the exact name, while others opt just to use the first initial or first few letters. If you want to follow this tradition but already have a first name you love, you can always choose a middle name that commemorates a loved one.

Naming After the Living

While it is not commonly accepted to name after the living in Judaism, the consensus amongst all other religions is that it is fine to name your child after someone who is alive. In fact, many consider it a great honor. If you have a parent, grandparent. aunt, uncle, or friend who has made a large impact on your life, you might consider using their name-- or a variation of it-- as the first or middle name of your baby.

Other Religious Traditions

Christianity seems to have the least concrete guidelines when it comes to religious customs involved with baby naming. The main rule in Judaism, as explained above, is that you should not name after the living. In Islam, it is frowned upon to give names with inappropriate or provocative meanings or using any variations of Allah's name or the names of false gods.

Following Family Traditions

Maybe your family has had a tradition for years that you'd like to follow, or maybe you just want to start your own tradition to be followed for generations to come. This could be everything from naming the first-born male in your family a certain name, to giving each child in your family the same initials. If your daughter's name is Rachel Amanda Smith, you might to want name your newborn son Ryan Adam Smith. This way, they both have the same initials, "RAS".

Following Local Customs

Depending on where you live, your options for baby names may be limited. In Germany, there is a list of names you must choose from. This is done to avoid confusing spellings, embarrassing names, and being unable to tell the child's gender just by looking at their name. Even if your options aren't legally limited, some countries have more popular traditions that are expected to be followed. For example, families in the United Kingdom are expected to choose more traditional names. Just look at Prince George and Princess Charlotte!

Any and all of these traditions are by no means necessary to follow. You can absolutely choose a name simply because you and your partner love the name. These are merely ideas to keep in mind if you're looking to follow a certain custom or tradition.

General Baby Naming Trends for 2017/2018

Alternate spellings are very on-trend right now. Instead of just seeing Riley, you might see Rylie, Ryleigh, and Reilly. Presley is a popular name, but so are alternate spellings like Preslee, Presleigh, and Preslie. Other examples are Kailey/Kailee/Kaylie/Kallie and Leah/Lia/Leuh/Leigha. For boys' names, Aiden is popular, but so are variations such as Aidan, Aydan, and Adin. Jason has been a top-ranking name amongst boys for years, but more people are branching out to name their sons Jayson, Jaysen, and Jaceson.

Vintage names are all the rage these days. Names that were popular fifty and seventy-five years ago are coming back in style. For guys, these are names like Oliver, Leo, Henry, and Martin. Some of the girls' names include Olive, Amelia, Nora, Eleanor, Hazel, and Stella. It's at the point where, if you hear someone calling for Lilian, you're not sure if they're calling for a grandmother or a toddler!

Naming after pop culture has now become the norm. Since the release of *Frozen*, Anna and Elsa have both skyrocketed up the list of popular baby girl names. The hit television show Pretty *Little Liars* breathed life back into names like Ezra, Aria, Caleb, and Spencer, while an alternate spelling of Aria (Arya) has also made its way into the mainstream courtesy of *Game of Thrones.*

Of course, as you might guess, people are naming their children not only after television characters, but also after celebrities themselves. Some examples of names inspired by iconic figures in the entertainment industry are Otis after Otis Redding, Lennon after John Lennon, and Audrey after Audrey Hepburn. Others choose to name after current Hollywood celebrities, like Adele, Lucy Hale from *Pretty Little Liars,* and Ian Somerhalder from *The Vampire Diaries*. Even celebrities name after celebrities, like Ashlee Simpson naming her child Jagger.

Last names as first names have never been as popular as they are now, used for both boys and girls. Some examples are:

- o Beckett
- o Carter
- o Parker
- o Reed
- o Lincoln
- o Kennedy
- o Anderson
- o Jameson
- o McKinley

Gender neutral names are more popular than ever. Instead of having names that are specifically for girls or boys, the wall is being torn down and people are using names that could be used for either gender or used to be predominantly used for the other gender. The top gender neutral baby names of 2017 so far include Quincy, Remi, Sasha, and Ray.

Names like Harper, Ashley, Kendall, and Payton were predominantly male names decades and centuries ago but are now thought of as female names. Other names like Riley and Morgan were formerly thought of as girl names but are also popular names for boys.

Place names as baby names have increased in popularity lately, both among celebrities and among the general population. Ashlee Simpson has a son named Bronx and Jill Duggar of *19 Kids and Counting* named her baby boy Israel. Reese Witherspoon's four-year-old son is named Tennessee.

Now other baby names inspired by places are making their way to the mainstream. For girls, these include Dakota, Vienna, Savannah, and Chandler, while boys are being given names like Dallas, Hudson, and Memphis.

How Baby Names Have Changed

Baby naming isn't what it used to be one hundred, fifty, or even ten years ago. Trends have changed, top names have changed, and the process by which people choose names have changed. Fifty years ago, people couldn't log on to a computer and look up names by first letter or meaning. They had to go with what they knew, which, in part, limited their choices. There were also different top names year after year, with some of them starting to cycle over again. Names like Eleanor, Clara, and Clementine were used more commonly in the early 1900s and are back on top. Eleanor has even been in the top sixty for girls' names for the past several years.

Did you know that the same names have comprised the top five for the girls for the past seven years? Or that 2016 was the first time in over 20 years that Jacob didn't make the top five for boys? We're going to run down the list of the five most popular boys' and girls' name for each of the past forty years, as collected by the United States Social Security Administration. Who knows? You might be inspired by a vintage name, and you'll probably be surprised to learn which names have been the most popular over the course of the last decade.

Girls' Names

1976: Jennifer, Amy, Melissa, Heather, Angela

1977: Jennifer, Melissa, Amy, Jessica, Heather

1978: Jennifer, Melissa, Jessica, Amy, Heather

1979: Jennifer, Melissa, Amanda, Jessica, Amy

1980: Jennifer, Amanda, Jessica, Melissa, Sarah

1981: Jennifer, Jessica, Amanda, Sarah, Melissa

1982: Jennifer, Jessica, Amanda, Sarah, Melissa

1983: Jennifer, Jessica, Amanda, Ashley, Sarah

1984: Jennifer, Jessica, Ashley, Amanda, Sarah

1985: Jessica, Ashley, Jennifer, Amanda, Sarah

1986: Jessica, Ashley, Amanda, Jennifer, Sarah

1987: Jessica, Ashley, Amanda, Jennifer, Sarah

1988: Jessica, Ashley, Amanda, Sarah, Jennifer

1989: Jessica, Ashley, Brittany, Amanda, Sarah

1990: Jessica, Ashley, Brittany, Amanda, Samantha

1991: Ashley, Jessica, Brittany, Amanda, Samantha

1992: Ashley, Jessica, Amanda, Brittany, Sarah

1993: Jessica, Ashley, Sarah, Samantha, Emily

1994: Jessica, Ashley, Emily, Samantha, Sarah

1995: Jessica, Ashley, Emily, Samantha, Sarah

1996: Emily, Jessica, Ashley, Sarah, Samantha

1997: Emily, Jessica, Ashley, Sarah, Hannah

1998: Emily, Hannah, Samantha, Sarah, Ashley

1999: Emily, Hannah, Alexis, Sarah, Samantha

2000: Emily, Hannah, Madison, Ashley, Sarah

2001: Emily, Madison, Hannah, Ashley, Alexis

2002: Emily, Madison, Hannah, Emma, Alexis

2003: Emily, Emma, Madison, Hannah, Olivia

2004: Emily, Emma, Madison, Olivia, Hannah

2005: Emily, Emma, Madison, Abigail, Olivia

2006: Emily, Emma, Madison, Isabella, Ava

2007: Emily, Isabella, Emma, Ava, Madison

2008: Emma, Isabella, Emily, Olivia, Eva

2009: Isabella, Emma, Olivia, Sophia, Ava

2010: Isabella, Sophia, Emma, Olivia, Ava

2011: Sophia, Isabella, Emma, Olivia, Ava

2012: Sophia, Emma, Isabella, Olivia, Ava

2013: Sophia, Emma, Olivia, Isabella, Ava

2014: Emma, Olivia, Sophia, Isabella, Ava

2015: Emma, Olivia, Sophia, Ava, Isabella

2016: Emma, Olivia, Ava, Sophia, Isabella

Boys' Names

1976: Michael, Jason, Christopher, David, James

1977: Michael, Jason, Christopher, David, James

1978: Michael, Jason, Christopher, David, James

1979: Michael, Christopher, Jason, David, James

1980: Michael, Christopher, Jason, David, James

1981: Michael, Christopher, Matthew, Jason, David

1982: Michael, Christopher, Matthew, Jason, David

1983: Michael, Christopher, Matthew, David, Joshua

1984: Michael, Christopher, Matthew, Joshua, David

1985: Michael, Christopher, Matthew, Joshua, Daniel

1986: Michael, Christopher, Matthew, Joshua, David

1987: Michael, Christopher, Matthew, Joshua, David

1988: Michael, Christopher, Matthew, Joshua, Andrew

1989: Michael, Christopher, Matthew, Joshua, David

1990: Michael, Christopher, Matthew, Joshua, Daniel

1991: Michael, Christopher, Matthew, Joshua, Andrew

1992: Michael, Christopher, Matthew, Joshua, Andrew

1993: Michael, Christopher, Matthew, Joshua, Tyler

1994: Michael, Christopher, Matthew, Joshua, Tyler

1995: Michael, Matthew, Christopher, Jacob, Joshua

1996: Michael, Matthew, Jacob, Christopher, Joshua

1997: Michael, Jacob, Matthew, Christopher, Joshua

1998: Michael, Jacob, Matthew, Joshua, Christopher

1999: Jacob, Michael, Matthew, Joshua, Nicholas

2000: Jacob, Michael, Matthew, Joshua, Christopher

2001: Jacob, Michael, Matthew, Joshua, Christopher

2002: Jacob, Michael, Joshua, Matthew, Ethan

2003: Jacob, Michael, Joshua, Matthew, Andrew

2004: Jacob, Michael, Joshua, Matthew, Ethan

2005: Jacob, Michael, Joshua, Matthew, Ethan

2006: Jacob, Michael, Joshua, Ethan, Matthew

2007: Jacob, Michael, Ethan, Joshua, Daniel

2008: Jacob, Michael, Ethan, Joshua, Daniel

2009: Jacob, Ethan, Michael, Alexander, William

2010: Jacob, Ethan, Michael, Jayden, William

2011: Jacob, Mason, William, Jayden, Noah

2012: Jacob, Mason, Ethan, Noah, William

2013: Noah, Jacob, Liam, Mason, William

2014: Noah, Liam, Mason, Jacob, William

2015: Noah, Liam, Mason, Jacob, William

2016: Noah, Liam, William, Mason, James

Baby Names by the Letter

If you're looking to follow a tradition that involves choosing a name for your child that starts with a certain letter, check out the list below. Here's a quick rundown of some awesome names that are known, but not so popular that people will roll their eyes and ask, "Another Emma?". Of course, there are tons of other options for each letter, but these are some favorites that will fit right in with the trends of 2017 and 2018.

Girls:

Adeline	Baylee	Eden
Addison	Callie	Eliza
Arabella	Cecilia	Evangeline
Ayla	Delaney	Fiona

Grace	Makayla	Sloan
Hadley	Mira	Teagan
Hailey	Natalia	Tessa
Hayden	Noelle	Ulla
Isabel	Norah	Uma
Ivy	Olive	Valerie
Jade	Opal	Vivian
Jordyn	Ophelia	Wyatt
Josie	Payton	Ximena
Keira	Quinn	Yasmin
Kimberly	Reese	Yvonne
Leia	Raelynn	Zara
Leora	Ryleigh	Zoe
Liliana	Selena	
Lyla	Sienna	

Boys:

Adam	Blake	Caden
Asher	Brody	Cash
Bennett	Bryce	Colin

Dawson	Logan	Timothy
Dean	Luca	Tristan
Elliott	Miles	Tucker
Everett	Micah	Uri
Finley	Nathanial	Uriel
Garrett	Oliver	Vincent
Hude	Preston	Wesley
Isaac	Quinn	Weston
Isaiah	Raphael	Xander
Jayce	Rhett	Yates
Jesse	Sasha	Zachary
Kenneth	Sawyer	Zayden
Killian	Sebastian	
Kyle	Tanner	

Trending Names 2017/2018

These are some of the most popular baby names of 2017, as compiled by Baby Center.

Girls:

Emma	Olivia	Ava

Sophia	Harper	Abigail
Mia	Aria	Evelyn
Charlotte	Ella	Chloe

Boys:

Liam	Oliver	Ethan
Noah	Benjamin	Aidan
Lucas	Jackson	Elijah
Mason	Logan	Michael

Baby Naming Checklist

Run down this checklist to make sure the name you're thinking about for your baby meets all—or at least most—of these criteria.

- Is it unique enough that they won't have three other children in their class with the same name?

- Does it hold meaning for you, your partner, and/or your families?

- Will people be able to pronounce the name?

- Have you checked to make sure the name doesn't have an unfortunate meaning or inappropriate initials?

- If you've opted for an alternate spelling for a common name, is it easy to understand and pronounce?

- If it is of importance to you, does the name hold a positive meaning?

If your answer to most of these questions is "no", you should probably go back and re-read the first few chapters!

Now let's look at names for boys and then for girls.

PART 2 Boy and Girl Names with Meaning and Origin

Boy names:

Aaden, little fiery one, American, Irish

Aarav, peaceful, Hindi

Aaron, high mountain; exalted, Hebrew

Aarush, first ray of sun, Hindi

Abdiel, servant of God, Hebrew

Abdullah, servant of Allah, Arabic

Abel, breath, Hebrew

Abraham, father of multitudes, Hebrew

Abram, high father, Hebrew

Ace, unity, Latin

Achilles, thin-lipped, Greek

Adam, son of the red earth, Hebrew

Adan, son of the red earth, Spanish

Aden, little and fiery, Irish

Adonis, lord, Greek

Adrian, man of Adria, Latin

Adriel, God is my master, Hebrew

Adrien, from Adria, French

Agustin, the exalted one, Latin

Ahmad, greatly praised, Arabic

Ahmed, greatly praised, Arabic

—**Aidan**, little and fiery, Irish

—**Aiden**, little and fiery, Irish

Alan, handsome; cheerful, Irish

Albert, noble; bright, German

Alberto, noble; bright, Germanic

Alden, old wise friend, English

Aldo, old and wise, Italian, German

Alec, defending men, Greek

Alejandro, defending men, Spanish

Alessandro, defending men, Italian

Alex, defending men, Greek

Alexander, defending men, Greek

Alexis, defender, Greek

Alexzander, defending men, Greek

Alfonso, noble; ready, Spanish, Italian

Alfred, wise counselor, English

Alfredo, wise counselor, Celtic

Ali, supreme; exalted, Arabic

Alijah, the Lord is my God, Hebrew

Allan, handsome; cheerful, Irish

Allen, handsome, Celtic

Alonso, "Adalfuns", Portuguese, Spanish

Alonzo, noble; ready, Italian

Alvaro, cautious, Spanish

Alvin, noble friend, English

Amare, handsome, African

Amari, eternal, Hebrew

Ameer, king; treetop, Arabic, Hebrew

Amir, king; treetop, Arabic, Hebrew

Amos, carried by God, Hebrew

Anakin, warrior, American

Anders, strong and manly, Scandinavian

Anderson, son of Anders, Scandinavian

Andre, man, French, Portuguese

Andres, manly, Spanish

Andrew, strong and manly, Greek

Andy, strong and manly, Greek

Angel, messenger, Greek

Angelo, messenger, Italian

Anson, son of Anne, English

Anthony, priceless one, Latin

Antoine, priceless one, French

Anton, priceless one, German, Scandinavian

Antonio, priceless one, Spanish, Italian

Apollo, manly beauty, Greek

Archer, bowman, English

Ares, ruin; bane, Greek

Ari, lion of God, Hebrew

Arian, warrior; honourable, Indo-Iranian

Ariel, lion of God, Hebrew

Arjun, bright; shining; white, Hindi

Arlo, barberry tree, Spanish

Armando, soldier, Spanish, Portuguese, Italian

Armani, freeman, Persian

Aron, enlightened; high mountain, Hebrew, Spanish

Arthur, bear, Celtic

Arturo, bear, Celtic

Aryan, warrior, Indo-Iranian

Asa, born in the morning, Hebrew

Asher, fortunate; happy one, Hebrew

Ashton, ash trees place, English

Atlas, a titan, Greek

Atticus, from Attica, Latin

August, great; magnificent, German

Augustine, great; magnificent, English

Augustus, great; magnificent, Latin

Austin, great; magnificent, English

Avery, ruler of the elves, English

Avi, father, Hebrew

Axel, father of peace, German

Axl, father of peace, Scandinavian

Axton, sword stone, English

Ayaan, God's gift, Arabic

Aydan, little fiery one, Irish

Ayden, little fiery one, Irish

Aydin, intelligent, Turkish

Azariah, helped by God, Hebrew

Barrett, bear strength, German

Baylor, one who delivers goods, English

Beau, handsome, French

Beckett, bee cottage, English, Irish

Beckham, homestead by the stream, English

Ben, son of, Hebrew

Benjamin, son of the right hand, Hebrew

Bennett, blessed, English

Benson, son of Ben, English

Bentlee, meadow with coarse grass, English

Bentley, meadow with coarse grass, English

Benton, bent grass enclosure, English

Billy, resolute protection, English

Bishop, overseer, English

Blaine, slender, Irish

Blaise, to lisp; stammer, French

Blake, fair-haired; dark, English

Blaze, one who stutters, Latin

Bo, to live, Swedish, Danish

Bobby, bright fame, English

Bode, shelter, Scandinavian

Boden, blonde; floor, Celtic, German

Bodhi, awakened, Sanskrit

Bodie, shelter; one who brings news, Scandinavian

Boone, a blessing, French

Boston, a place name, English

Bowen, son of Owen, Celtic

Braden, from Bradden, dweller near the broad valley, English

Bradley, dweller at the broad road, English

Brady, spirited, Irish

— **Braeden**, broad and wide, Celtic

Braiden, broad valley, English

Brandon, from the beacon hill, English

Branson, sword, Germanic

Brantlee, fiery torch, English

Brantley, fiery torch, English

Braxton, Brock's settlement, English

Brayan, noble and virtuous, American, Celtic

Brayden, broad, English

— **Braydon**, broad, English

Braylen, from the name Braydon and Lyn, American

Braylon, from the name Braydon and Lyn, American

Brecken, little freckled one, Irish

Brendan, prince, Irish

Brenden, prince, Irish

Brennan, brave, Gaelic

Brent, high place, English

Brentley, hilltop, Celtic

Brett, a native of France or England, English

Brian, strong and virtuous, Irish

Briar, a thorny patch, Word name

Brice, freckled, Scottish

Briggs, from the village near a bridge, English

Brixton, Brixton district of London, English

Brock, badger, English

Brodie, little ridge, Scottish

Brody, ditch, Scottish

Bronson, son of brown-haired one, English

Brooks, of the brook, English

Bruce, from the brushwood thicket, Scottish, English

Bruno, brown, German

Bryan, strong and virtuous, Irish

Bryant, strong and virtuous, Irish

Bryce, freckled, Scottish

Brycen, son of Brice, English

Bryson, son of Brice, English

Byron, barn for cows, English

Cade, round; barrel, English

Caden, companion of friend; warrior, Arabic, English

Caiden, fighter, Gaelic

Cain, spear; possessed, Hebrew

Cairo, victorious, Arabic

— **Caleb**, devotion to God, Hebrew

— **Callan**, battle; rock, Gaelic

Callen, rock, Gaelic

Callum, dove, Scottish, Latin

Calvin, hairless, Latin

Camden, winding valley, Scottish

Camdyn, winding valley, Scottish

Cameron, crooked nose, Scottish

Camilo, young ceremonial attendant, Latin

Camren, crooked nose, Scottish

Camron, crooked nose, Scottish

Canaan, merchant, Hebrew

Cannon, clergyman, English

Carl, free man, German

Carlos, free man, Spanish

Carmelo, cultivated terrain, Spanish

Carson, son of the marsh-dwellers, Irish, Scottish

Carter, transporter of goods by cart, English

Case, observant, Irish

Casen, descendant of cathasach; pure, Irish, Scandinavian

Casey, brave in battle, Irish

Cash, wealthy man, English

Cason descendant of cathasach; pure, Irish, Scandinavian

Cassius, hollow, Latin

Castiel, my cover is God, Hebrew

Cayden, fighter, Gaelic

Cayson, courageous and tough, Irish

Cedric, bounty, Celtic

Cesar, long haired Spanish, Latin

Chace, huntsman, English

Chad, protector, English

Chaim, life, Hebrew

Chance, good luck, English

Chandler, candle maker, French

Channing, young wolf, English

Charles, free man, French

Charlie, free man, English

— **Chase**, dweller of the hunting ground, English

Chevy, knight, French

Chris, carrier of Christ, Greek

Christian, follower of Christ, Greek

Christopher, carrier of Christ, Greek

Clark, scribe, English

Clay, mortal, Teutonic

Clayton, mortal, English

Clyde, from the name of Scottish Clyde river, Scottish

Cody, helpful, Irish

Coen, bold advisor, Dutch

Cohen, priest, Hebrew

Colby, from the dark village, American

Cole, swarthy coal black, English

Coleman, dove, Irish

Colin, young pup, Scottish, Irish

Collin, young pup, Scottish, Irish

Colt, from the dark town, English

Colten, coal town, English

Colton, from the dark town, English

Conner, much desire, Irish

Connor, strong willed, Irish

Conor, lover of hounds, Irish

Conrad, brave counsel, German

Cooper, barrel maker, English

Corbin, raven, Latin

Corey, seething pool, Scottish

Cory, seething pool, Scottish

Craig, dwells at the crag, Scottish

Crew, dam-like structure, Welsh

Cristian, follower of Christ, Spanish

Cristiano, follower of Christ, Italian, Portoguese

Cristopher, bearer of Christ, Greek

Crosby, village with crosses, Irish

Cruz, cross, Portuguese

Cullen, handsome, Gaelic

Curtis, courteous, French

Cyrus, throne, Persian

Dakota, friend, Native American

Dallas, wise, Gaelic

Dalton, the settlement in the valley, English

Damari, gentle, Latin

Damian, to tame, Greek

Damien, one who tames, French

Damon, gentle, Greek

Dane, brook, English

Dangelo, from the angel, Italian

Daniel, God is my judge, Hebrew

Danny, God has judged, Scottish

Dante, enduring, Latin

Darian, gift, Greek

Dariel, open, French

Dario, wealthy, Greek

Darius, preserver, Persian

Darrell, open, French

Darren, great, Gaelic

Darwin, dear friend, English

Dash, from Chiel, English

Davian, beloved, American

David, beloved, Hebrew

Davin, dearly loved, Hebrew

Davion, beloved, English

Davis, David's son, English

Dawson, David's son, English

Dax, a town in south-western France, French

Daxton, reference to the French town Dax, English

Dayton, day town, English

Deacon, dusty one, English

Dean, church official, English

Deandre, combination of prefix De and Andre, American

Deangelo, from the angel, Italian

Declan, man of prayer, Irish

Demetrius, of Demeter, Latin

Dennis, from Dionysius (mythical God of wine), English

Denver, from Anvers, English, French

Derek, the peoples ruler, English

Derrick, gifted ruler, English

Deshawn, God is gracious, African American

Desmond, from South Munster, Gaelic

Devin, poet, Irish

Devon, poet, Irish

Dexter, right handed, Latin

Diego, supplanter, Spanish

Dilan, like a lion, Irish

Dillon, like a lion, Irish

Dimitri, earth-lover, Greek

Dominic, belonging to the lord, Latin

Dominick, of the Lord, Latin

Dominik, belonging to the lord, Slavic, German

Dominique, of the lord, French

Donald, great chief, Scottish

Donovan, brown-haired chieftain, Irish

Dorian, of Doris, a district of Greece, Greek

Douglas, dark water, Scottish

Drake, dragon, Greek

Draven, of the raven, American

Drew, manly, Scottish

Duke, English rank of nobility, English

Duncan, dark warrior, Scottish

Dustin, a fighter, English

Dwayne, dark, Irish

— **Dylan**, son of the wave, Welsh

Ean, the Lord is gracious, Scottish

Easton, from East town, English

Eddie, rich in friendship, English

Eden, delight, Hebrew

Edgar, fortunate and powerful, English

Edison, son of Edward, English

Eduardo, wealthy guardian, English

Edward, wealthy guardian, English

Edwin, wealthy friend, English

Eli, my God, Hebrew

Elian, the Lord is my God, Hebrew, Welsh

Elias, Yaweh is God, Hebrew

Elijah, Yaweh is God, Hebrew

Eliseo, God is salvation, Italian, Spanish

Elisha, God is salvation, Hebrew

Elliot, Jehovah is God, Greek

Elliott, Jehovah is God, Greek

Ellis, Jehovah is God, Greek

Emanuel, God with us, Hebrew

Emerson, brave; powerful, German

Emery, brave; powerful, German

Emiliano, work, Italian, Spanish

Emilio, industrious, Latin

Emmanuel, God is with us, Hebrew

Emmet, universal, English, German

–**Emmett**, universal, English, German

–**Emmitt**, universal, English, German

Emory, brave, English

Enoch, dedicated, Hebrew

Enrique, rules his household, Spanish

Enzo, winner, Italian

Ephraim, fruitful; productive, Hebrew

Eric, eternal ruler, Norse

Erick, ruler of the people, Norse

Erik, ever kingly, Scandinavian

Ernest, serious and determined, German

Ernesto, serious and determined, Spanish

Esteban, crowned in victory, Spanish

Ethan, strong, Hebrew

Eugene, wellborn, Greek

Evan, young, Welsh

Everett, brave as a wild boar, English

Ezekiel, God strengthens, Hebrew

Ezequiel, God strengthens, Spanish, Portuguese

Ezra, help, Hebrew

Fabian, bean grower, Latin

Felipe, friend of horses, Spanish

Felix, happy, Latin

Fernando, adventurer, Spanish

Finley, fair-haired hero, Irish, Scottish

Finn, fair, Irish

Finnegan, fair, Irish

Finnley, fair warrior, Irish

Fisher, fisherman, English

Fletcher, arrow maker, English

Flynn, son of the red-haired one, Irish

Ford, dweller at the ford, English

Forrest, dweller near the woods, English

Francis, Frenchman or free man, Latin

Francisco, Frenchman or free man, Spanish

Franco, Frenchman or free man, Spanish

Frank, Frenchman or free man, French

Frankie, Frenchman or free man, French

Franklin, free born landowner, English

Freddy, peaceful ruler, German

Frederick, peaceful ruler, German

Gabriel, man of God, Hebrew

Gael, stranger, Irish, American

Gage, oath; pledge, French

Gannon, fair-skinned and fair-haired, Irish

Garrett, spear strength, Irish

Gary, hard or bold spear, English

Gauge, pledge, French

Gavin, white hawk, Celtic

George, farmer, Greek

Gerald, ruler with the spear, English

Gerardo, spear courageous, Spanish

Giancarlo, God's gracious gift, Italian

Gianni, God is gracious, Italian

Gibson, Gilbert's son, English

Gideon, hewer; having a stump for a hand, Hebrew

Gilbert, shining pledge, German

Giovani, God is gracious, Italian

Giovanni, God is gracious, Italian

Gordon, great hill, Scottish

Grady, noble and illustrious, Irish

Graham, gravelly homestead, Scottish

Grant, large, Scottish

Graysen, the son of the bailiff, English

— **Grayson**, the son of the bailiff, English

Gregory, vigilant; a watchman, Greek

Grey, gray-haired, English

Greyson, son of Gregory, American

Griffin, strong lord, Welsh

Guillermo, resolute protector, Spanish

✦ **Gunnar**, bold warrior, Scandinavian

✦ **Gunner**, battle strong, Swedish

Gustavo, royal staff, Spanish

Haiden, fire, English

Hamza, sour leaves, Muslim

Hank, estate ruler, German

Harlan, from the hare's land, English

Harley, hare clearing, English

Harold, army ruler, Scandinavian

Harper, harpist; minstrel, English

Harrison, son of Harry, English

Harry, estate ruler, English

Harvey, battle worthy, French

Hassan, handsome, Muslim

Hayden, from the hedged in valley, English

Hayes, hedged area, English

Heath, untended land where flowering shrubs grow, English

Hector, holding fast, Greek

Hendrix, estate ruler, Dutch, German

Henrik, estate ruler, Danish, Hungarian

Henry, estate ruler, German

Hezekiah, God is my strength, Hebrew

Holden, from the hollow in the valley, English

Houston, from Hugh's town, Scottish

Hudson, Hugh's son, English

Hugh, intellect, English

Hugo, intellect, Latin

Hunter, one who hunts, English

Huxley, inhospitable place, English

Ian, the Lord is gracious, Scottish

Ibrahim, a prophet's name, Muslim

Ignacio, fiery, Spanish

Iker, visitation, Basque

Immanuel, God is with us, Hebrew

Isaac, laughter, Hebrew

Isaiah, salvation of the Lord, Hebrew

Isaias, God's helper, Hebrew

Ishaan, the sun, Hindi

Ismael, God listens, Hebrew

Israel, may God prevail, Hebrew

Issac, laughter, Hebrew

Ivan, gracious gift from God, Russian

Izaiah, God is salvation, Hebrew

Jabari, brave, Egyptian

Jace, a healing, Greek

Jack, God is gracious, English

Jackson, God is gracious, Scottish

Jacob, supplanter, Hebrew

Jacoby, supplanter, Hebrew

Jaden, Jehovah has heard, Hebrew

Jadiel, God has heard, Spanish

Jadon, thankful, Hebrew

Jagger, carter, English

Jaiden, God has heard, Hebrew

Jaime, supplanter, Spanish

Jairo, Jehovah enlightens, Spanish

Jake, he grasps the heel, Hebrew

Jakob, supplanter, Hebrew

Jalen, from James and Lenore, American

Jamal, handsome, Arabic

Jamari, handsome, American

Jamarion, grace, American

James, supplanter, English

— **Jameson**, son of James, English

Jamie, supplanter, Hebrew

Jamir, handsome, Arabic

— **Jamison**, supplanter, English

Jared, descending, Hebrew

Jase, a healing, Greek

Jasiah, God supports, Hebrew

Jason, a healing, Greek

Jasper, bringer of treasure, Persian

Javier, bright, Spanish

Javion, elaboration of Javon, American

Javon, "Greece", Hebrew

Jax, God has been gracious, English

Jaxen, son of Jack, English

Jaxon, Gid has been gracious, English

Jaxson, son of Jack, English

Jaxton, a product of American imagination, American

Jay, to rejoice, English

Jayce, a healing, Greek

Jayceon, one who makes people feel better, Greek

Jayden, thankful, Hebrew

Jaydon, Jehovah has heard, Hebrew

Jaylen, jaybird, American

Jayson, a healing, Greek

Jayvion, offers advice, Hebrew

Jaziel, chosen by God, Hebrew

Jedidiah, beloved of the Lord, Hebrew

Jefferson, son of Geoffrey, English

Jeffery, traveller, German

Jeffrey, traveller, German

Jensen, son of Jens, English

Jeremiah, may Jehovah exalt, Hebrew

Jeremy, may Jehovah exalt, Hebrew

Jermaine, brotherly, Latin

Jerome, holy name, Greek

Jerry, may Jehovah exalt, Hebrew

Jesse, wealthy, Hebrew

Jessie, wealthy, Hebrew

Jesus, Jehovah is salvation, Latin

Jett, free, American

Jimmy, supplanter, Hebrew

Joaquin, God will judge, Spanish

Joe, may Jehovah add, Hebrew

Joel, Jehovah is his God, Hebrew

Joey, may Jehovah add, Hebrew

Johan, God is gracious, German

John, Jehovah has been gracious, Hebrew

Johnathan, Jehovah has give, Hebrew

Johnny, Jehovah's gift, Hebrew

Jon, Jehovah has been gracious, English

Jonael, honest, Hispanic

Jonah, dove, Hebrew

Jonas, gift from God, Hebrew

Jonathan, Jehovah has given, Hebrew

Jonathon, gift of Jehovah, Hebrew

Jordan, to flow down, Hebrew

Jordy, down flowing, Hebrew

Jordyn, flowing down, Hebrew

Jorge, farmer, Spanish

Jose, may God give increase, Spanish

Joseph, may Jehovah add, Hebrew

Joshua, Jehovah is generous, Hebrew

Josiah, Jehovah has healed, Hebrew

Josue, God is salvation, Hebrew

Jovani, form of Jovan 'Father of the sky', Latin

Joziah, Jehovah has healed, Hebrew

Juan, God is gracious, Spanish

Judah, praised, Hebrew

Jude, praised, Latin

Judson, descend, Hebrew

Juelz, modern invented name, American

Julian, youthful, Latin

Julien, youthful, French

Julio, youthful, Latin

Julius, downy-bearded, Latin

Junior, younger, Latin

Justice, righteous, Latin

Justin, just, Latin

Justus, upright, Biblical

Kade, from the wetlands, Gaelic

Kaden, companion, Arabic

Kaeden, fighter, Gaelic

Kai, sea, Hawaiian

Kaiden, battler, American

Kaison, rebel, American

~ **Kaleb**, brave, Hebrew

Kalel, friend, Arabic

Kamari, moonlight, African

Kamden, winding valley, Scottish

Kamdyn, winding valley, Scottish

Kameron, crooked nose, Scottish

Kamren, modern variant of Cameron for girls, English

Kamron, crooked nose, Scottish

Kamryn, modern variant of Cameron for girls, English

Kane, warrior, Celtic

Kannon, form of Kuan-yin who was Chinese Buddhist, Japanese

Kareem, generous, Arabic

Karson, a follower of Christ, English

Karter, transporter of goods by cart, English

Kase, belonging to Case, French

Kasen, helmeted, Latin

Kash, hollow, American

Kashton, makes friends easily, American

Kason, house, American

Kayden, son of Cadan, Irish

Kaysen, a contemporary name, American

Kayson healer, American

Keagan, a thinker, Irish

Keaton, place of hawks, English

Keegan, a thinker, Irish

Keenan, ancient, Irish

Keith, dwells in the woods, Welsh

Kellan, slender, German, Irish

Kellen, slender, German, Irish

Kelvin, river man, English

Kendall, royal valley, English

Kendrick, greatest champion, Welsh

Kenneth, handsome, Scottish

Kenny, handsome, Irish

Kevin, handsome by birth, Irish

Khalil, companion, Arabic

Kian, ancient, Irish

Kieran, dark skinned, Gaelic

Killian, war strife or church, Irish

King, king, English

Kingsley, from the king's meadow, English

Kingston, from the king's village, English

Knox, from the hills, English

Kobe, tortoise, Swahili

Kody, helpful, English

Kohen, priest, Hebrew

Kolby, dark-haired, German

Kole, swarthy, English

Kolten, coal town, German

Kolton, coal town, German

Konnor, lover of hounds, Irish

Korbin, crow, Latin

Kristian, follower of Christ, English

Kristopher, form of Christopher, Scandinavian

Kye, rejoice, Latin

Kylan, a place name referring to the narrows, Gaelic

Kyle, a place name referring to the narrows, Gaelic

Kylen, a place name referring to the narrows, Gaelic

Kyler, a place name referring to the narrows, Gaelic

Kymani, adventurous traveller, Eastern African

Kyree, Lord, Greek

Kyrie, Lord, Greek

Kyson, son of Kyle, English

Lachlan, warlike, Scottish

Lamar, of the sea, French

Lance, land, French

Landen, long hill, English

⁓ **Landon**, long hill, English

Landry, ruler, French, English

Landyn, long hill, English

Lane, from the long meadow path, English

Langston, from the long enclosure, English

Larry, of Laurentum, Latin

Lawrence, of Laurentum, Latin

Lawson, son of Lawrence, English

Layne, roadway, English

Layton, settlement with a leek garden, Old English

Leandro, lion-made, Spanish, Portuguese, Italian

Lee, meadow or wood, English

Legend, story, English, Latin

Leighton, herb garden, English

Leland, from the meadow land, English

Lennon, lover, Irish

Lennox, with many elm trees, Scottish

Leo, lion, Latin

Leon, lion, French

Leonard, brave lion, German

Leonardo, lion-bold, Portuguese

Leonel, young lion, Spanish

Leonidas, lion, Latin

Leroy, the king, French

Levi, attached, Hebrew

Lewis, renowned warrior, English

Liam, resolute protection, Irish

Lincoln, Roman colony at the pool, English

Lionel, young lion, French

Lochlan, from the fjord-land, Scottish

Logan, small hollow, Scottish

London, fortress of the moon, Latin

Lorenzo, from the place of laurel trees, Spanish

Louie, famous warrior, French

Louis, famous warrior, French

Luca, man from Lucania, Italian

Lucas, man from Lucania, Latin

Lucca, man from Lucania, Italian

Lucian, form of Luke; illumination, American

Luciano, form of Luke; illumination, American

Luis, famous fighter, German

Luka, light, Latin

Lukas, light, Latin

Luke, light giving, Greek

Lyric, of the lyre, French

Mack, son of, Celtic

Madden, little dog, Irish

Maddox, son of Maddock, Welsh

Magnus, greatest, Latin

Maison, house, French

Major, greater, Latin

Makai, toward the sea, Hawiian

Malachi, my messenger, Hebrew

Malakai, my messenger, Hebrew

Malaki, my messenger, Hebrew

Malcolm, devotee of St. Colombia, Scottish

Malik, master, Arabic

Manuel, God is with us, Hebrew

Marc, derived from Latin Marcus, English

Marcel, form of the Latin Marcellus, French

Marcelo, hammer, Italian

Marco, Mars (Roman God of war), Italian

Marcos, of Mars, Portuguese

Marcus, hammer, Latin

Mario, hammer, Latin

Mark, warlike, Latin

Markus, of Mars, German

Marley, pleasant seaside meadow, English

Marlon, little falcon, French

Marquis, title name ranking below duke and above earl, French

Marshall, love of horses, Scottish

Martin, of Mars, Latin

Marvin, from the sea fortress, Welsh

Mason, worker in stone, English

Mateo, God's gift, Spanish

Mathew, gift of God, Hebrew

Mathias, gift of God, Aramaic

Matias, gift of God, Spanish, Finnish

Matteo, gift of God, Hebrew, Italian

Matthew, gift of God, Hebrew

Matthias, gift from God, Hebrew

Maurice, dark-skinned, Latin

Mauricio, dark-skinned, Spanish

Maverick, independent, American

Max, greatest, English, German

Maxim, the greatest, Latin

Maximilian, greatest, Latin

Maximiliano, the greatest, Italian

Maximo, the greatest, Italian

Maximus, greatest, Latin

Maxton, greatest, English

Maxwell, Magnus' spring, Scottish

Mayson, worker in stone, English

Mekhi, who is like God, Hebrew

Melvin, chief, Irish

Memphis, enduring and beautiful, Greek, Coptic

Messiah, anointed one, Hebrew

Micah, who is like the Lord, Hebrew

Michael, gift from God, Hebrew

Micheal, who is like God, Gaelic

Miguel, who is like God, Portuguese

Milan, gracious, Stavic

Miles, soldier or merciful, English

Miller, grinder of grain, English

Milo, soldier, Latin, Old German

Misael, as God is, Hebrew

Mitchell, gift from God, Hebrew

Mohamed, glorified, Arabic

Mohammad, praiseworthy, Arabic

Mohammed, glorified, Arabic

Moises, from the water, Spanish

Morgan, bright sea, Welsh

Moses, delivered from the water, Egyptian

Moshe, delivered from the water, Hebrew

Muhammad, praiseworthy, Arabic

Musa, a prophet's name, Muslim

Mustafa, chosen, Muslim

Myles, destroyer, Greek

Nash, by the ash tree, English

Nasir, supporter, Muslim

Nathan, gift from God, Hebrew

Nathanael, gift of God, Biblical

Nathaniel, gift of God, Biblical

Nehemiah, comforted by God, Hebrew

Neil, champion, Gaelic

Nelson, son of the champion, Irish

Neymar, unknown meaning, Brazilian

Nicholas, people of victory, Greek

Nickolas, victorious, Slavic

Nico, victorious, English

Nicolas, people's victory, Greek

Niko, victorious, English

Nikolai, victory of the people, East Slavic

Nikolas, victorious, Slavic

Nixon, victorious, English

Noah, comfort, Hebrew

Noe, consolation, Biblical

Noel, Christmas, French

Nolan, champion, Irish

Oakley, from the oak tree, English

Odin, wealthy, Anglo-Saxon

Oliver, the olive tree, English

Omar, eloquent, Hebrew

Omari, God the highest, African

Orion, rising in the sky, Greek

Orlando, famous land, Spanish

Oscar, divine spear, English

Osvaldo, divine power, Teutonic

Otis, wealthy, German

Otto, born eighth or wealthy, German

Owen, young warrior, Welsh

Pablo, small, Spanish

Parker, keeper of the forest, English

Patrick, noble, English

Paul, small, Latin

Paxton, from the peaceful farm, English

Payton, noble, Irish

Pedro, the merchant of Venice, American

Peter, a rock, English

Peyton, royal, Scottish

Philip, lover of horses, Greek

Phillip, lover of horses, Greek

Phoenix, bird reborn from its own ashes, Greek

Pierce, form of Piers from Peter, Irish

Porter, gatekeeper, French

Preston, priest's town, English

Prince, principal one, English

Princeton, principal one, Latin

Quentin, born fifth, Latin

Quincy, born fifth, Latin

Quinn, counsel, Gaelic

Quintin, fifth, Latin

Quinton, born fifth, Latin

Rafael, God has healed, Hebrew

Raiden, thunder and lightning, Japanese

Ramon, form of Raymond 'Guards wisely, Spanish

Randy, house wolf, English

Raphael, God has healed, Hebrew

Rashad, thinker, Arabic

Raul, form of Ralph 'wolf counsel', Spanish

Ray, guards wisely, German

Rayan, land lush and rich in water, Arabic

Rayden, no meaning, American

Raylan, modern twist on Raymond, American

Raymond, wise protector, Teutonic

Reagan, regal, Celtic

Reece, ardent, English

Reed, redheaded, English

Reese, fiery, Welsh

Reginald, powerful ruler, German

Reid, redheaded, Scottish

Remington, from the raven farm, English

Remy, rower, French

Rene, reborn, French

Reuben, the vision of the son, Biblical

Rex, king, Latin

Rey, king, Spanish

Reyansh, ray of light, Hindi

Rhett, fiery, Welsh

Rhys, ardour; rashness, Welsh

Riaan, little king, Hindi

Ricardo, strong ruler, Spanish

Richard, powerful; strong ruler, German

Ricky, gifted ruler, English

Ridge, from the ridge, English

Riley, valiant, Gaelic

River, riverbank, Old French

Robert, bright; shining, German

Roberto, bright; shining, Portuguese

Robin, bright; shining, German

Rocco, rock, Italian

Rocky, rock, English

Rodney, island of reeds, English

Rodolfo, famous wolf, Spanish

Rodrigo, famous ruler, Portuguese

Rogelio, famous soldier, Spanish

Roger, farmed spear, English

Rohan, ascending, Sanskrit

Roland, renowned in the land, English

Rolando, renowned in the land, French

Roman, man of Rome, Latin

Romeo, a pilgrim to Rome, Italian

Ronald, mighty counsellor, Scottish

Ronan, oath, Celtic

Ronin, little seal, Irish

Ronnie, mighty counsellor, Scottish

Rory, red, Irish

Rowan, red, Gaelic

Rowen, red haired, Irish

Roy, red haired, Celtic

Royal, red, Gaelic

Royce, royal, English

Ruben, behold a son, Hebrew

Rudy, famed wolf, German

Russell, red haired, Latin

Ryan, kingly, Irish

Ryder, knight, American

Ryker, hardy power, Danish

Rylan, island meadow, Irish

— **Ryland**, from the rye land, English

Sage, wise one, English

Salvador, savior, Spanish

Salvatore, savior, Italian

Sam, sun child, Hebrew

Samir, jovial, Muslim

Samson, bright sun, Hebrew

Samuel, heard by God, Hebrew

Santana, place name, Spanish

Santiago, named for Saint James, Spanish

Santino, little saint, Italian

Santos, saint, Spanish

Saul, inquired for God, Hebrew

Sawyer, cuts timber, Celtic

Scott, from Scotland, English

Seamus, form of James; supplanter, Gaelic

Sean, gift from God, Irish

Sebastian, venerable, Latin

Sergio, attendant, Italian

Seth, anointed, Hebrew

Shane, God is gracious, Irish

Shaun, God is gracious, Irish

Shawn, gift from God, Irish

Shiloh, the one to whom it belongs, Hebrew

Silas, of the forest, Latin

Simon, snubnosed, Greek

Sincere, earnest, American

Skylar, phonetic spelling of Schuyler, English

Skyler, phonetic spelling of Schuyler, English

Solomon, peace, Hebrew

Sonny, son, American

Soren, strict, Scandinavian

Spencer, keeper of provisions, American

Stanley, stone leigh, Old English

Stefan, crowned with laurels', Russian

Stephen, crown, Greek

Sterling, pure, English

Stetson, nickname for a boxer, Anglo-Saxon

Steve, victorious, Greek

Steven, crown, English

Sullivan, dark eyes, American

Sutton, from the south farm, English

Sylas, wood or forest, English

Talon, claw, English

Tanner, worker in leather, English

Tate, he who talks too much, Native American

Tatum, brings joy, English

Taylor, tailor, English

Terrance, Roman clan name, Latin

Terrell, thunder ruler, English

Terrence, smooth, Latin

Terry, powerful, Germanic

Thaddeus, praise, Aramaic

Thatcher, roofer, English

Theo, God given, Greek

Theodore, God-given, Greek

Thiago, supplanter, Spanish

Thomas, twin, Aramaic

Timothy, God's honour, Greek

Titan, defender, Greek

Titus, pleasing, Biblical

Tobias, from the Hebrew Tobiah, Spanish

Toby, abbreviation of Tobias, English

Todd, fox, English

Tomas, twin, Gaelic

Tommy, twin, Aramaic

Tony, highly praiseworthy, English

Trace, brave, Anglo-Saxon

Travis, crossroads, English

Trent, refers to English river Trent, English

Trenton, refers to the English river Trent, English

Trevor, prudent, Irish

Trey, three, English

Tripp, traveler, English

Tristan, outcry, French

Tristen, outcry, Arthurian

Triston, outcry, French

Troy, derives from ancient Greek city of Troy, English

Truman, loyal, English

Tucker, Tucker of doth, English

Turner, lathe worker, English

Ty, earth, English, Irish

Tyler, tile layer, English

Tyrone, from Owen's territory, Irish

Tyson, son of a German, French

Ulises, Greek name Odysseus, Spanish

Uriah, God is my light, Hebrew

Uriel, God is my light, Hebrew

Urijah, the Lord is my light or fire, Biblical

Wade, river crossing, English

Valentin, strong, Spanish

Valentino, brave or strong, Italian

Walker, worker in cloth, English

Walter, powerful ruler, German

Van, equivalent of 'de' in French names, Dutch

Vance, marshland, English

Warren, protector, German

Vaughn, little, Welsh

Waylon, land beside the road, English

Wayne, craftsman, English

Wesley, from the west meadow, English

Westin, west town, English

Weston, west town, English

Vicente, conquering, Portuguese

Victor, conqueror, Latin

Vihaan, dawn, Sanskrit

Wilder, wild, American

Will, will-helmet, German

William, resolute protector, German

Willie, will-helmet, German

Wilson, son of Will, English

Vincent, conquering, Latin

Vincenzo, conqueror, Latin

Winston, from a friend's town, English

Vivaan, full of life, Hindi

Wyatt, guide, English

Xander, defending men, Greek

Xavier, new house or bright, Basque, Arabic

Xzavier, new house or bright, Arabic

Yadiel, God has heard, Spanish

Yahir, he will enlighten, Hebrew, Arabic

Yahya, a prophet's name, Muslim

Yehuda, praised, Hebrew

Yosef, God shall add, Hebrew

Yousef, God increases, Arabic

Yusuf, God increases, Arabic

Zachariah, Jehovah has remembered, Hebrew

Zachary, Remembered by God, Hebrew

Zackary, God has remembered, Hebrew

Zaid, he shall add, Egyptian

Zaiden, lucky one, Hebrew

Zain, beauty, Muslim

Zaire, the river that swallows all rivers, African-American

Zander, to defend, Latin

Zane, gift from God, Hebrew

Zavier, new house, Basque, Spanish

Zayden, little fire, Celtic, American

Zayn, grace, Arabic

Zayne, grace, Arabic

Zechariah, Jehovah has remembered, Hebrew

Zeke, God strengthens, Hebrew

Zion, monument, Biblical

Girl names:

Aaliyah, highborn, Arabic

Abby, father's joy, Hebrew

Abigail, my father is joyful, Hebrew

Abril, symbolizes spring, Spanish

Ada, nobility, French

Adaline, noble, Teutonic

Adalyn, noble, French

Adalynn, noble, French

Addilyn, noble, French

Addilynn, noble, French

Addison, son of Adam, Old English

Addisyn, son of Adam, American, Scottish

Addyson, form of Addison; son of Adam, English

Adelaide, nobility, French

Adele, kind and tender, Germanic

Adelina, noble, Italian, Spanish, Portuguese

Adeline, pleasant, German

Adelyn, nobility, German

Adelynn, nobility, German

Adilynn, nobility, German

Adley, judicious, Hebrew

Adriana dark, Latin

Adrianna, dark, French

Adrienne, the dark one, French

Aileen, light, Irish

Aimee, dearly loved, French

Ainsley, one's own meadow, Scottish

Aisha, life, Muslim

Aislinn, dream, Irish

Aitana, the glorious one, Portuguese

Aiyana, eternal blossom, Native American

Alaia, joyful, Basque

Alaina, harmony, Irish

Alana, little rock, Irish

Alani, dear child, Irish

Alanna, child, Gaelic

Alannah, little rock, Irish

Alaya, dwelling, Sanskrit

Alayah, heavens, Arabic

— **Alayna**, dear child, Irish

Aleah, God's being, Arabic, Persian

Aleena, good-looking, Celtic

Alejandra, defender of mankind, Spanish

Alena, light, Greek

Alessandra, defender of men, Greek

Alexa, defending men, Greek

Alexandra, defending men, Greek

Alexandria, defending men, Greek

Alexia, helper, Greek

Alexis, defender, Greek

Alia, supreme, Arabic

Aliana, my God has answered, Hebrew

Alianna, my God has answered, Hebrew

Alice, nobility, French

Alicia, nobility, Latin

Alina, noble, German

Alisha, protected by God, Sanskrit

Alison, noble, Norman French

Alissa, noble humor, Teutonic

Alisson, noble, French

Alivia, olive tree, Latin

Aliya, heavens, Arabic

Aliyah, highest social standing, Muslim

Aliza, joy, Hebrew

Allie, harmony, Celtic

Allison, noble, Scottish

Ally, harmony, Celtic

Allyson, noble, Scottish

Alma, kind, Latin

Alondra, defender of mankind, Spanish

Alyson, honest, Irish

Alyssa, rational, Greek

Amalia, hard working, Italian

Amanda, lovable, Latin

Amani, wishes, American

Amara, grace or bitter, Igbo, Latin

Amari, eternal, Hebrew

Amaris, given by God, Hebrew

Amaya, night rain, Spanish

Amber, powerful and complete, American

Amelia, work, German

Amelie, hard working, French

America, land of the prince, Latin

Amia, beloved, French

Amina, trustworthy, Muslim

Aminah, trustworthy, Arabic

Amira, princess; one who speaks, Hebrew

Amirah, princess; one who speaks, Hebrew

Amiya, delight, Indian

Amiyah, delight, Indian

Amy, dearly loved, French

Amya, no meaning, American

Ana, grace, Spanish

Anabella, beautiful; graceful, Latin

Anabelle, loving, French

Anahi, the immaculate, Spanish

Analia, combination of Ana and Lucia, Spanish

Anastasia, resurrection, Greek

Anaya, answer of God, Hebrew

Andi, brave, English

Andrea, manly, Greek

Angel, messenger or angel, Greek

Angela, messenger or agel, Greek

Angelica, like an angel, Latin

Angelina, messenger or angel, Greek

Angeline, messenger or angel, Greek

Angelique, like and angel, French

Angie, messenger or angel, Greek

Anika, sweetness or face, Nordic

Aniya, God has shown meaning, Polish

Aniyah, ship, Hebrew

Ann, merciful, English

Anna, grace, Hebrew

Annabel, loving, Scottish

Annabella, beautful; graceful, Latin

Annabelle, loving, Scottish

Annalee, biblical, Latin

Annalise, graced with God's bounty, Latin

Anne, favour or grace, Hebrew

Annie, frequently used as an independent name, English

Annika, gracious, Swedish

Ansley, clearing with a hermitage, English

Anya, grace, Russian

April, symbolizes spring, Latin

Arabella, derived from 'orabilis' meaning yeilding to prayer, Latin

Aranzaamong the thorns, Basque

Arden, valley of the eagle, English

Arely, lion of God, American, Hebrew, Spanish

Aria, lioness, Italian, Hebrew

Ariadne, most holy, Greek

Ariah, most holy, Greek

Ariana, holy, Latin

Arianna, holy, Latin

Ariel, sprite; lion of God, Hebrew

Ariella, lion of God, Hebrew

Arielle, lion of God, Hebrew

Ariya, lioness, Hebrew

Ariyah, lioness, Hebrew

Armani, castle, Hebrew

Arya, noble goddess, Indian

Aryana, most holy, Italian

Aryanna, most holy, Italian

Ashley, lives in the ash tree grove, English

Ashlyn, dream, Irish

Ashlynn dream, Irish

Asia, muddy; boggy, Biblical

Aspen, aspen tree, American, English

Astrid, godly strength, Scandinavian

Athena, goddess of wisdom, Greek

Aubree, rules with elf-wisdom, French

Aubrey, blond ruler; elf ruler, French

Aubrianna, combination of Aubrey and Anna, American

Aubrie, rules with elf-wisdom, English

Aubriella, combination of Aubrey and Ella, American

Aubrielle, elf ruler, American

Audrey, noble strength, English

Audrina, noble strength, English

Aurelia, the golden one, Latin

Aurora, Roman goddess of the dawn, Latin

Autumn, born in the fall, English

Ava, life, Latin

Avah, life, Latin

Avalyn, beautiful breath of life, Old English

Avalynn, beautiful breath of life, Old English

Averi, ruler of the elves, English

Averie, ruler of the elves, English

Avery, ruler of the elves, English

Aviana, bird, Latin

Avianna, bird, Latin

Aya, to fly swiftly, Hebrew

Ayla, oak tree, Hebrew

Ayleen, bright shining light, Irish

Aylin, moon halo, Turkish

Azalea, dry, Greek

Azaria, helped by God, Hebrew

Azariah, helped by God, Hebrew

Bailee, steward; bailiff, English

Bailey, public official, English

Barbara, from the Greek barbarous meaning foreign or strange, English

Baylee, steward; bailiff, English

Beatrice, she who brings happiness, Latin

Belen, arrow, Greek

Bella, beautiful; lovable; graceful, Latin

Bethany, the house of song, Biblical

Bianca, white; shining, Italian

Blair, from the fields, Irish

Blake, kight; dark, English

Blakely, from the light meadow; from dark meadow, English

Bonnie, pretty; charming, Scottish

Braelyn, primrose, American

Braelynn, primrose, American

Braylee, no meaning, American

Breanna, strong and virtuous, American

Brenda, sword or torch, Scottish

Brenna, beacon on the hill Little raven, Irish

Bria, hill, Irish

Briana, strong and virtuous, American

Brianna, strong and virtuous, American

Briar, a thorny patch, English

Bridget, the high one oe strength, Irish

Briella, God is my strength, Hebrew

Brielle, hunting grounds, French

Briley, woodland, American

Brinley, burnt wood, English

Bristol, a place name, English

Brittany, originally the ancient duchy of Bretagne in France, English

- **Brooke**, lives by the stream, English

Brooklyn, water, English

Brooklynn, water, English

Bryanna, strong, Celtic

Brylee, combination of Bryan and Lee, American

Bryleigh, combination of Bryan and Leigh, American

Brynlee, hill; mound, Welsh

Brynn, hill, Welsh

Cadence, a rhythmic flow of sounds, English

Caitlin, pure; clear, French

Caitlyn, meaning pure, Irish

Cali, most beautiful, Greek

Callie, most beautiful, Greek

Cameron, crooked nose, Scottish

Camila, free-born, Latin

Camilla, servant for the temple, Latin

Camille, French form of Camilla or Camillus, French

Camryn, crooked nose, Scottish

Cara, beloved, Italian

Carla, Germanic form of Charles meaning a man, German

Carlee, free man, American

Carly, free man, American

Carmen, garden, Spanish

Carolina, strong, Latin

Caroline, strong, Italian

Carolyn, strong, Italian

Carter, transporter of goods by cart, English

Casey, from a polish word meaning 'proclamation of peace', English

Cassandra, unheeded prophetess, Greek

Cassidy, intelligent, Irish

Cataleya, flower name, English

Catalina, from the Greek Catherine meaning pure, Portuguese

Catherine, pure, French

Caylee, slender, Gaelic

Cecelia, blind, Latin

Cecilia, blind, Latin

Celeste, based on the Latin caelestis meaning heavenly, French

Celia, heavenly, Latin

Celine, Latin 'caelum' meaning sky or heaven, French

Chana, graceful, Hebrew

Chanel, canal; channel, French

Charlee, manly, English

Charleigh, free man, English

Charley, from Old English 'ceorl' meaning man, English

Charli, manly, English

Charlie, manly, English

Charlize, free man, English

Charlotte, free man, French

Chaya, life, Hebrew

Chelsea, seaport, English

Cherish, to treasure and care for, English, Old French

Cheyenne, an Algonquian tribe of the Great Plains, French

Chloe, green shoot; fresh blooming, Greek

Christina, follower of Christ, Latin

Christine, follower of Christ, French

Ciara, saint of dark, American

Claire, bright; clear, French

Clara, bright or clear, Latin

Clare, illustrious, Latin

Clarissa, gentle; famous, English

Claudia, lame, French

Clementine, from 'Clemens', meaning mild or peaceful, Latin

Colette, necklace, French

Collins, abbreviation of Nicolas meaning people's victory, English

Cora, girl or maiden, Greek

Coraline, from the coral of the sea, Greek

Cordelia, daughter of the sea, Latin, Celtic

Corinne, maiden, French

Courtney, from the court or short nose, French

Crystal, gem name, Scottish

Cynthia, of Cynthus, Greek

Dahlia, from the valley, Norse

Daisy, Day's eye, English

Dakota, friend; ally, Native American

Dalary, modern invented name, American

Daleyza, delightful, Spanish

Dallas, from the waterfall, Gaelic

Dana, from Denmark, English

Danica, morning star, Slavic

Daniela, God is my judge, Hebrew

Daniella, God has judged, Hebrew

Danielle, God is my judge, French

Danna, feminine God will judge, English

Daphne, bay tree or laurel tree, Greek

Dayana, divine, Latin

Deborah, bee, Hebrew

Delaney, competitor's child; from the river Slaney, Irish

Delilah, amorous; temptress, Hebrew

Demi, abbreviation of Demetria-mythological goddess of harvest, English

Denise, feminine form of Dennis, French

Desiree, desired, French

Destiny, certain fortune; fate, English

Diana, fertile, Latin

Dixie, refers to French word for ten, English

Dorothy, gift of God, English

Dulce, sweet, Latin

Dylan, born near the sea, Welsh

Eden, delight, Hebrew

Edith, happy warfare, English

Eileen, from a surname meaning hazelnut, French

Elaina, shining light, French

Elaine, bright shining light, Old French

Eleanor, shining light, American

Elena, bright one, Spanish

Eliana, Jehovah is God, Hebrew

Elianna, God has answered me, Latin

Elin, most beautiful woman, Welsh

Elisa, consecrated to God, Spanish

Elisabeth, oath of God; God is satisfaction, Hebrew

Elise, oath of God, Greek

Eliza, oath of God, Greek

Elizabeth, God is satisfaction, Greek

Ella, beautiful fairy, English

Elle, beautiful fairy, English

Ellen, courage, Anglo-Saxon

Elliana, my God has answered, Latin

Ellie, most beautiful woman, English

Elliot, Jehovah is God, Greek

Elliott, Jehovah is God, Greek

Ellis, Jehovah is God, Greek

Ellison, son of elder, English

Eloise, famous in war, French

Elora, the crown of victory, English

Elsa, oath of God, Greek

Elsie, my God is bountiful; God is plenty, Scottish

Elyse, from the blessed isles, Greek

Ember, hot ashes, English

Emelia, industrious; striving, Latin

Emely, rival, Latin

Emerie, industrious, German

Emerson, Emery's son; brave, German

Emersyn, son of Emery, English

Emery, industrious, German

Emilee, striving, Latin

Emilia, industrious, Italian

Emilie, striving, Latin

Emily, industrious, Latin

Emma, whole, German

Emmalee, industrious, Latin

Emmaline, hardworking, French

Emmalyn, combination of Emma and Lyn, English

Emmalynn, combination of Emma and Lynn, English

Emmeline, industrious, French

Emmy, hardworking, German

Emory, brave; powerful, English

Erica, ever kingly, Scandinavian

Erika, eternal ruler, Norse

Erin, peace; poetic name for Ireland, Gaelic

Esme, esteemed; emerald, French, Persian

Esmeralda, the emerald gemstone, Spanish

Esperanza, hope, Spanish

Estella, star, French

Estelle, star, Latin

Esther, refers to the planet Venus; star, Persian

Estrella, star, Spanish

Eva, living one, Latin

Evalyn, form of Evelyn; life, English

Evangeline, bringer of good news, Greek

Eve, lively, Hebrew

Evelyn, hazelnut, French

Evelynn, hazelnut, French

Everleigh, from Ever's meadow, English

Everly, from Ever's meadow, English

Evie, lively, Hebrew

Faith, confidence, Greek *middle*

Farrah, happy, Arabic

Fatima, captivating, Arbabic

Faye, fairy, French

Felicity, happiness; good luck, Latin

Fernanda, adventurous, German

Finley, fair hero, Irish

Fiona, white or fair, Gaelic

Frances, free one, Latin

Francesca, free one, Italian

Frankie, free one, French

Freya, lady, Scandinavian

Frida, beautiful, Norse

Gabriela, God's able-bodied one, Hebrew

Gabriella, woman of God, Italian

Gabrielle, woman of God, French

Galilea, a rolled sheet, Italian

Gemma, jewel or gem, Italian

Genesis, beginning, Biblical

Genevieve, of the race of women, German

Georgia, tiller of the soil or farmer, English

Gia, God is gracious, Italian

Giana, God is gracious, Italian

Gianna, God is gracious, Italian

Giavanna, God is kind, Italian

Giovanna, God is kind, Italian

Giselle, pledge, German

Giuliana, young, Italian

Gloria, glory, Latin

Grace, God's favour, English middle

Gracelyn, combination of Grace and Lyn, American, English

Gracelynn, combination of Grace and Lynn, American, English

Gracie, favour; blessing, Latin

Greta, pearl, Swedish

Guadalupe, wolf valley, Arabic

Gwen, mythical son of Gwastad, Celtic

Gwendolyn, blessed; white browed, Welsh

Hadassah, myrtle or bride, Persian

Hadlee, heather field, English

Hadleigh, heather field, English

Hadley, heather field, English

Hailee, Hay's meadow, English, Scottish

Hailey, Hay's meadow, English, Scottish

Haley, ingenious, Irish

Halle, little rock, Norse

Hallie, from the Hall, English

Hana, blossom, Japanese

Hanna, grace, Hebrew

Hannah, grace, Hebrew

Harlee, the long field, English

Harley, the long field, English

Harlow, meadow of the hares, English

Harmoni, unity, Latin

Harmony, concord, Latin

Harper, harpist; ministrel, English

Hattie, rules the home, English

Haven, place of shelter; safety, English

Hayden, from the hedged in valley, English

Haylee, hay clearing, English

Hayley, hay field, English

Hazel, hazel tree nut; nut-bearing shrub, English

Heather, a flowering evergreen in Scotland, English

Heaven, heaven, English

Heavenly, little lady, English

Heidi, nobility, French

Helen, the bright one, Greek

Helena, shining light, Greek

Henley, high meadow, English

Holland, wooded land, Dutch

Holly, from the plant name; holy, English

middle **Hope**, one of the Christian virtues, English

Hunter, one who hunts, English

Iliana, from Ilium or Troy, Greek

Imani, faith, Arabic

Ingrid, fair; beautiful, Norse

Ireland, place name, English

Irene, peace, Greek

Iris, bringer of joy, Latin

Isabel, my God is beautiful, Latin

Isabela, God of plenty, Spanish

Isabella, devoted to God, Hebrew

Isabelle, devoted to God, Hebrew

Isla, from the name of a Scottish river, Scottish

Itzel, rainbow lady, Mayan

Ivanna, gift from God, Hebrew

Ivory, white; pure, English

Ivy, faithfulness, English

Izabella, devoted to God, Hebrew

Jacqueline, supplanter, French

Jada, knowledgeable one, Hebrew

Jade, jewel, Spanish

Jaelyn, supplanter, American

Jaelynn, supplanter, American

Jaida, the gemstone jade; the color green, English

Jaliyah, no meaning, American

Jamie, supplanter, Hebrew

Jane, Jehovah has been gracious, English

Janelle, God is gracious, English

Janessa, God is gracious, Scottish, Norwegian

Janiya, from Jana, Hebrew

Janiyah, from Jana, Hebrew

Jasmin, a flower name; French

Jasmine, a flower name, Persian

Jaycee, phonetic name based on initials, English

Jayda, knowledgeable one, American, Hebrew

Jayde, the color green, English

Jayden, Jehovah has heard, Hebrew

Jayla, to ascend, Hebrew

Jaylah, to ascend, Hebrew

Jaylee, no meaning, American

Jayleen, beautiful jay bird, American

Jaylene, feminine, American

Jaylin, beautiful jay bird, American

Jaylynn, feminine, English

Jazlyn, combination of Jocelyn and the musical term jazz, English

Jazlynn, combination of Jocelyn and musical term jazz, English

Jazmin, flower name, Persian

Jazmine, flower name, Persian

Jemma, dove, Hebrew

Jenna, white shadow; white wave, English

Jennifer, fair one, Arthurian Legend

Jenny, God has been gracious, English

Jessa, short form of Jessica, Hebrew

Jessica, rich, Hebrew

Jessie, wealthy, Hebrew

Jewel, jewel, French

Jillian, child of the gods, English

Jimena, heard, Spanish

Joanna, God is gracious, Latin

Jocelyn, one of the Goths, German

Jocelynn, medieval name adopted as a feminine name, French

Johanna, gift from God, Hebrew

Jolene, compound of Jo and feminine name element – ene, English

Jolie, cheerful, French

Jordan, the river of judgement, Biblical

Jordyn, descend, American

Jordynn, descend, American

Joselyn, member of the Gauts tribe, German

Josephine, may Jehovah add, French

Josie, may Jehovah add, French

Joslyn, medieval male name adopted as feminine name, French

Journee, trip, American

Journey, trip, American

Joy, rejoicing, French

Joyce, cheerful, English

Judith, jewess, Hebrew

Julia, young, Latin

Juliana, youthful, Latin

Julianna, young; Jove's child, Latin

Julianne, downy grace, Latin

Julie, downy, French

Juliet, youthful, French

Julieta, from Julian; Jove's child, Spanish

Juliette, youthful, French

Julissa, descended from Jove, French

June, young, Latin

Juniper, an evergreen tree, English, Latin

Justice, upright; righteous, Latin

Kadence, falling; rhythm and flow, American, English

Kaelyn, keeper of the keys; pure, American

Kaelynn, keeper of the keys; pure, English

Kai, the sea, Hawiian

Kaia, the sea, Hawiian

Kailani, sea and sky, Hawaiian

Kailee, keeper of the keys; pure, English

Kailey, keeper of the keys; pure, English

Kailyn, pure; English

Kairi, sea, American

Kaitlyn, form of Caitlin from Catherine meaning pure, Irish

Kaitlynn, form of Caitlin from Catherine meaning pure, Irish

Kaiya, forgiveness, Japanese

Kalani, the sky; cheiftain, Hawaiian

Kali, black, Indian

Kaliyah, ornament; bright one, African American

Kallie, from the forest, Irish

Kamila, perfect, Arabic

Kamryn, modernused for girls, English

Kara, dear; beloved, Italian

~~**Karen**,~~ pure, Greek

Karina, pure, English

Karla, womanly; strength, Scandinavian

Karlee, womanly; strength, German

Karlie, womanly, Scandinavian

Karsyn, son of the marsh dwellers, Scottish, Irish

Karter, one who transports goods in a cart, English

Kassandra, unheeded prophetess, Greek

Kassidy, curly-headed, English

Katalina, pure, Greek

Kate, pure; clear, Latin

Katelyn, pure, English

Katelynn, pure, English

Katherine, pure, Latin

Kathleen, pure, Greek

Kathryn, clear; pure, Latin

Katie, pure; clear, Irish

Kaya, my elder sister, Native American, Hopi

Kayden, son of Caden; battle, English

Kaydence, falling; rhythm, American, English

Kayla, keeper of the keys; pure, English

Kaylee, pure, English

Kayleigh, pure; keeper of the keys, English

Kaylie, keeper of the keys; pure, English

Kaylin, keeper of the keys; pure, English

Kaylynn, keeper of the keys; pure, English

Keira, dusky; dark-haired, Irish

Kelly, war; lively, Irish

Kelsey, from the ship's land, Norse

Kendall, royal valley, English

Kendra, knowledge, English

Kenia, form of Kenya, Hebrew

Kenley, from the king's meadow, English

Kenna, born of fire, Scottish

Kennedi, misshapen head, Irish

Kennedy, helmeted, Irish

Kensington, the town of Cynsige's People, English

Kensley, spring glade, English, Nordic

Kenya, yes to God, Hebrew

Kenzie, good-looking, American, Scottish

Keyla, pure; English

Khaleesi, modern invented name, American

Khloe, young green shoot, English

Kiana, ancient, Irish

Kiara, dark, Irish

Kiera, dark-haired, Irish

Kiley, a wood or church, Gaelic

Kimber, royal fortress, Anglo-Saxon

Kimberly, from the wood of the royal forest, English

Kimora, brave and noble, Japanese

Kinley, fair skinned warrior, Gaelic, Scottish

Kinslee, land of the king, English

Kinsley, king's field, English

Kira, light, Russian

Kora, maiden, Greek

Kori, God's peace; spear, Germanic, Celtic, Gaelic

Kristen, follower of Cgrist, Latin

Kristina, Follower of Christ, Latin

Kyla, feminine of Kyle, Gaelic

Kylee, feminine of Kyle, Gaelic

Kyleigh, feminine of Kyle, Gaeilc

Kylie, feminine of Kyle, Gaelic

Kyndall, royal valley, English

Kynlee, respelling of Kinley, American

Kyra, enthroned, Greek

Lacey, surname, Irish

Laila, born at night, Arabic

Lailah, born at night; sweetheart, Muslim

Lainey, ray of light, English, Welsh

Lana, derived from Irish Gaelic word for child, Gaelic

Landry, ruler, Anglo-Saxon

Laney, path; roadway, English

Lara, cheerful, Russian

Laura, laurel tree or sweet bay tree, Latin

Laurel, laurel, Latin, American

Lauren, of Laurentum, Latin

Lauryn, from Laurentum, Latin

Layla, born at night, Egyptian

Laylah, night; nocturnal, Arabic

Lea, derived from Hebrew Leah, Spanish

Leah, tired, Hebrew

Leanna, derived from an Irish Gaelic of Helen, English

Leia, child of heaven; heavenly flowers, Hawaiian

Leighton, her garden, English

Leila, born at night, Persian

Leilani, heavenly flower, Hawaiian

Lena, temptress, Russian

Lennon, little cloak, Gaelic

Lennox, lives near the place abounding in elm trees, Gaelic

Leona, lioness, French

Leslie, Scottish surname and place name, Scottish

Lexi, man's defender, Greek

Lexie, man's defender, Greek

Leyla, born at night, Arabic

Lia, bearer of good news; dependent, Greek, Hebrew, Italian

Liana, youthful, Latin

Libby, God's promise, English

Liberty, free, American

Lila, lilac; born at night, Persian

Lilah, feminine of Lyle: from the island, English

Lilia, purity and beauty, Latin

Lilian, derived from the flower name Lily; innocence, English

Liliana, lily, American

Lilianna, innocence; purity, Latin

Lilith, night monster, Hebrew

Lillian, innocence and beauty, English

Lilliana, purity; beauty, Latin

Lillianna, purity; beauty, Latin

Lillie, innocence; purtiy, English

Lilly, purity; beauty, English

Lily, pure; English

Lilyana, God is my oath, English

Lilyanna, combination of Lily and Anna, English

Lina, tender, Muslim

Linda, snake; lime tree, German

Lindsay, from the island of the lime tree, Scottish

Lindsey, from the island of the lime tree, Scottish

Lisa, oath of God, Hebrew

Liv, life, Scandinavian

Livia, life, English

Lizbeth, oath of God, Hebrew

Logan, from the hollow, Gaelic

Lola, sorrow, Spanish

London, place name, English

Londyn, respelling of London, Celtic

Lorelai, temptress, German

Lorelei, temptress, German

Louisa, famous warrior, Latin

Lucia, graceful light, Italian

Luciana, light, Latin

Lucille, French light, French

Lucy, light, Latin

Luna, the moon, Latin

Luz, seperation; an almond, Biblical

Lydia, woman from Lydia, Greek

Lyla, from the island, English

Lylah, amusement; dark beauty, American, Arabic, English

Lyra, lyre; lyrical, Greek

Lyric, of the lyre; song, French

Mabel, beautiful; lovable, Latin

Maci, derived from medieval form of Matthew, English

Macie, derived from medieval form of Matthew, English

Mackenzie, fair; favoured one, Scottish

Macy, derived from medieval male form of Matthew, French

Madalyn, from the tower, Hebrew

Madalynn, bitter, Spanish

Maddison, mighty battle, English

Madeleine, woman of Magdala, French

Madeline, woman of Magdala, French

Madelyn, high tower, Greek

Madelynn, high tower, Greek

Madilyn, high tower, Greek

Madilynn, high tower, Greek

Madison, derived from Matthew 'gift of God', English

Madisyn, derived from Matthew 'gift of God', English

Madyson, derived from Matthew ' gift of God', English

Mae, May, French

Maeve, joy, Irish

Maggie, pearl, Greek

Magnolia, flower, French

Maia, May, French

Maisie, pearl' child of light, Scottish

Makayla, who is like God, English

Makenna, happy one, Eastern African

Makenzie, comely; good-looking, Celtic, Gaelic, Scottish

Malaya, free, Filipino

Malaysia, land of mountains, American

Maleah, bitter, Hawaiian

Malia, bitter, Hawaiian

Maliah, bitter, Hawaiian

Maliyah, bitter, Hawaiian

Mallory, unfortunate; ill fated, French

Mara, bitter, English

Margaret, pearl, Greek

Margot, pearl, French

Maria, rebellion, Latin

Mariah, bitter, English

Mariam, bitter, Arabic

Mariana, bitter, Latin

Marianna, bitter, Latin

Marie, rebellion; wished for-child, Hebrew

Marilyn, rebillion; bitter, Hebrew

Marina, from the sea, Latin

Marisol, Mary soledad; Mary alone, Latin

Marissa, of the sea, Latin

Mariyah, the Lord is my teacher, Latin

Marjorie, pearl, Greek

Marlee, pleasant seaside meadow, English

Marleigh, pleasant seaside meadow, English

Marley, pleasant seaside meadow, English

Martha, lady, Aramaic

Mary, wished-for child; rebellion, Hebrew

Maryam, bitter, Greek

Matilda, strength in battle, German

Maya, daughter of Atlas, Latin

Mckenna, beloved of Aodh(Celtic god of fire), Celtic, Gaelic, Irish

Mckenzie, the fair one, Scottish

Mckinley, son of the white warrior; learned ruler, Gaelic

Meadow, grassy field, American

Megan, pearl, Greek

Meilani, heavenly beautiful, Hawaiian

Melanie, the black one, Latin

Melany, the black one, Latin

Melina, honey, Greek

Melissa, bee, Greek

Melody, music, Greek

Meredith, guardian of the sea, Welsh

Mia, commonly-used; wished-for child, Latin

Miah, mine; bitter, Swedish

Micah, gift from God, Hebrew

Michaela, gift from God, English

Michelle, close to God, Hebrew

Mikaela, gift from God, English

— **Mikayla**, gift from God, English

Mila, industrious, Czechoslovakian

Milan, gracious, Slavic

Milana, gracious, Slavic

Milani, from Milan, Italian

Milania, gracious, Greek

Milena, people's love, Russian

Millie, mild of strength, English

Mina, love, German

Mira, worthy of admiration; wonderful, Latin

Miracle, wonder, Latin

Miranda, wonderful, Latin

Miriam, rebellious, Hebrew

Miya, three arrows; temple, Japanese

Molly, bitter, English

Monica, alone; advisor, Greek

Monroe, from the red swamp, Gaelic

Monserrat, a mountain in Spain, Latin

Montserrat, jagged mountain, American

Morgan, bright sea, Welsh

Moriah, the Lord is my teacher, Hebrew

Mya, beloved, Egyptian

Myah, water, Greek

Myla, merciful, English

Myra, pour out; weep, Biblical

Nadia, hope, Slavic

Nala, olive, Latin

Nancy, grace, Hebrew

Naomi, pleasant, Hebrew

Natalee, birthday; especially birthday of Christ, French

Natalia, born at Christmas, Russian

Natalie, born at Christmas, French

Nataly, born at Christmas, French

Natasha, born at Christmas, Russian

Nathalia, birthday; especially birthday of Christ, French

Nathalie, birthday; especially birthday of Christ, French

Nathaly, birthday; especially birthday of Christ, French

Naya, brilliance, Swahili

Nayeli, I love you, Zapotec

Neriah, light; lamp of the Lord, Biblical

Nevaeh, heaven spelled backwards, American

Nia, brilliance, Swahili

Nicole, people's victory, Greek

Nina, favour grace, English

Noa, movement, Hebrew

Noelle, birthday, French

Noemi, pleasantness, Spanish

Nola, feminine of Nolan(noble), Gaelic

Noor, light, Arabic

Nora, abbreviation of Ealeanora 'light' and Honora 'honor', English

Norah, honour, Latin

Nova, new; young, Latin

Nyla, winner, African America, Arabic

Nylah, winner, African American, Arabic

Oakley, from the oak-tree meadow, English

Olive, symbol of peace, Latin

Olivia, olive branch, Latin

Ophelia, hemp; serpentine, Greek

Paige, attendant, French

Paislee, church; cemetery, English

Paisley, church, cemetery, Scottish

Paityn, fighting man's estate, English

Paloma, dove, Spanish

Paola, small, Latin

Paris, place name, Greek

Parker, keeper of the forest, English

Patricia, regal; noble, Latin

Paula, small, Latin

Paulina, small, Latin

Payton, fighting man's estate, English

Pearl, precious, Latin

Penelope, bobbin, Greek

Penny, flower; bobbin, Greek

Perla, precious, Spanish

Peyton, fighting man's estate, English

Phoebe, the shining one, Greek

Phoenix, bird reborn from its own ashes, Greek

Piper, piper, English

Presley, from the priest's meadow, English

Princess, royal son, American

Priscilla, ancient, Latin

Quinn, counsel, Gaelic

Rachel, ewe, Hebrew

Raegan, impulsive, Irish

Raelyn, well advised protector, American

Raelynn, well advised protector, American

Raina, queen, French

Raquel, innocent, Hebrew

Raven, raven, English

Rayna, queen, Hebrew

Reagan, regal, Celtic

Rebecca, captivating; knotted cord, Hebrew

Rebekah, captivating; knotted cord, Hebrew

Reese, ardent; fiery, Welsh

Regina, queen, Spanish

Reina, queen, Spanish

Remi, rower, French

Remington, from the raven farm, English

Remy, rower, French

Renata, reborn, Latin

Reyna, queen, Spanish

Rhea, the mother of the Greek god Zues, Greek

Riley, surname, Irish

River, riverbank, Latin

Rivka, captivating, Hebrew

Romina, from the land of the Christians, Arabic

Rory, red, Irish

Rosa, rose, Italian

Rosalie, rose, Latin

Rose, flower, Scottish

Roselyn, red haired, French

Rosemary, bitter rose, Latin

Rosie, rose, Latin

Rowan, red, Gaelic

Royal, red, Gaelic

Ruby, precious jewel, Latin

Ruth, companion, Hebrew

Ryan, kingly, Irish

Ryann, little king, Irish

Rylan, island meadow, Irish

Rylee, couageous, Irish

Ryleigh, courageous, Irish

Rylie, courageous, Irish

Sabrina, from Cyprus or from the river Severn, Latin

Sadie, mercy, Spanish

Sage, wise one, English

Saige, wise one, English

Salma, peace; perfection, Biblical

Samantha, listener, Aramaic

Samara, protected by God, Hebrew

Sandra, defender of men, Greek

Saniyah, radiant, Arabic

Sara, princess, Hebrew

Sarah, princess, Hebrew

Sarahi, my princess, Hebrew

Sarai, my lady, Biblical

Sariah, my lady, Biblical

Sariyah, my lady, Biblical

Sasha, defender of men, Russian

Savanna, from the open plain, Spanish

Savannah, from the open plain, Spanish

Sawyer, cuts timber, Celtic

Saylor, rope maker, Germanic

Scarlet, red, English

Scarlett, red, English

Scarlette, red, English

Selah, to praise, Hebrew

Selena, moon goddess, Greek

Serena, serene, Italian

Serenity, serene; calm, French

Sharon, from the Plain of Sharon, Hebrew

Shayla, question, Hebrew

Shelby, from the manor house 'Willow farm', English

Shiloh, the one to whom it belongs, Hebrew

Sidney, wide island, English

Siena, from Siena, Latin

Sienna, name of a city in Italy, Italian

Sierra, dark, Irish

Simone, heard, French

Sky, cloud, Norse

Skye, Isle of Skye, English

Skyla, sheltering, Dutch

Skylar, phonetic spelling of Schuyler, English

Skyler, phonetic spelling of Schuyler, English

Sloan, warrior, Gaelic

Sloane, warrior, Gaelic

Sofia, wise, Greek

Sophia, wise, Greek

Sophie, wise, Greek

Stella, derived from 'stella' meaning star, French

Stephanie, crown; victorious, Greek

Stevie, victorious, Greek

Summer, born during the summer, English

Susan, graceful lily, Hebrew

Sutton, from the south farm, English

Sydney, from Saint-Denis, French

Sylvia, from the forest, Latin

Tabitha, beauty; grace, Hebrew

Talia, dew of heaven, Hebrew

Taliyah, dew of heaven, Hebrew

Tara, where the kings met, Irish

Tatiana, feminine of Roman family clan name Tatius, Russian

Tatum, brings joy, English

Taya, valley field, Japanese

Taylor, tailor, English

Teagan, good-looking, Irish

Tegan, good-looking, Irish

Tenley, town, English

Teresa, name of saints 'Teresa of Avila' and 'Teresa of Lisieux', Spanish

Tessa, born fourth, Greek

Thalia, joyous muse of comedy, Greek

Thea, goddess, Greek

Tiana, uncertain, English

Tiffany, manifestation of God, Latin

Tinley, hedge; fence, English

Tori, triumphant, English

Trinity, three in one, Latin

Valentina, brave, Latin

Valeria, brave, Latin

Valerie, brave, Latin

Vanessa, butterfly, Greek

Veda, understanding, Sanskrit

Wendy, literary, English

Vera, faith; true, Russian

Veronica, true image, Latin

Whitney, from the white island, Anglo-Saxon

Victoria, victory; triumphant, Latin

Vienna, from Wine Country, American

Willa, valiant protector, English

Willow, slender; graceful, English

Winter, year, Anglo-Saxon

Violet, flower, Italian

Virginia, virgin, Spanish

Vivian, lively, Latin

Viviana, enchantress of Merlin, Latin

Vivienne, lively, French

Wren, ruler, Welsh

— **Wynter**, born in the winter, English *middle*

Ximena, one who hears, Spanish

Yamileth, beautiful, Spanish

Yareli, lady of the water, Spanish

Yaretzi, you will always be loved, Aztec

Yaritza, water lady, Spanish

Yasmin, jasmine flower, Arabic

Zahra, white, Arabic

Zainab, daughter of the Prophet Muhammad, Muslim

Zaniyah, forever always, Aztec

Zara, Eastern splendour; princess, Arabic

Zaria, flower or sunrise, Arabic

Zariah, blooming flower or sunrise, Arabic

Zariyah, flower or sunrise, Arabic

Zaylee, flower, Australian

Zelda, grey battle; Christian battle, German

Zendaya, give thanks, Shona

Zion, monument; raised up, Biblical

Zoe, life; alive, Greek

Zoey, life, Greek

Zoie, life, Greek

Zuri, white and lovely, French

Conclusion

There you have it—a complete guide to avoid every mishap or oversight that you could possibly encounter on the journey to choosing your baby's name. Enjoy this special time in your life, and give your child the rock star name that he or she deserves!